Mongolia

A Rhyming Journey Through a Land of Blue Sky

by Paul Fahidi

Mongolia
A Rhyming Journey Through a Land of Blue Sky

Copyright © 2025 Paul Fahidi

First published in Britain by
Seronok Books Limited
Liverpool, the United Kingdom

www.seronokbooks.com

ISBN 978-0-9933304-6-9

All rights reserved. No part of this publication may be reproduced, stored in a retrieval system or transmitted in any form by any means, electronic, mechanical, photocopying, recording or otherwise, without the written permission of Seronok Books Limited and the author.

The right of Paul Fahidi to be identified as the author and illustrator of this work, has been asserted by him in accordance with the Copyright, Designs and Patents Acts, 1988.

Paul Fahidi taught at an international school in Mongolia for four years. He travelled extensively across the country.

Learn about Mongolia from someone who has lived there!

Монгол улсын талаар монголд амьдарч байсан хүнээс мэдэж аваарай.

Mongol ulsyn talaar mongold amidarch baisan khünees medej avaarai.

A large landlocked country in the Asia of the east,

It's population compared to size in the world is the least.

The biggest city of Mongolia in English means "red hero,"

Ulaanbaatar is the coldest capital, where in winter it's subzero.

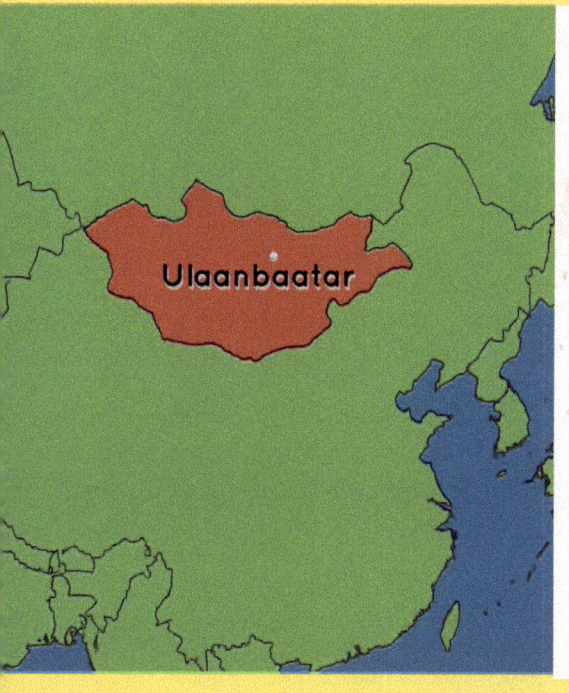

Rolling hills and green steppes run
across this large, rugged land,

And in the Gobi you can play
with two humped camels in the sand.

Nomads roam the steppes in their
cars, horses and gers,

This last of these is a round tent,
made of wood and animal hairs.

"Sain Uu" (**сайн үү**) is how you say hello,

But be careful, there is something you should know.

Show respect when you speak to many or a few,

Mongolians will say, "bayarlalaa" (**баярлалаа**) that means "thank you."

A deel for men and women are traditional Mongolian clothes,

They cover you from your neck, all the way to your toes.

Looking like a flashy coat, tightly fit for the girls,

More loose fitting for the boys... give us all some twirls.

There are various types of deels for different uses.

Mongolian traditional clothes

Deels that are used everyday are made from cotton or wool.

deel

Deels made for a special event or holiday are made from silk.

Mongolian khorkhog and tsuivan are two delicious dishes,

Barbecued food and beefy steam noodles, will meet all your wishes.

Buuz is a steam dumpling, it's ever so nice,

While khushuur is a fried meat pocket, a carnivores paradise.

buuz   khushuur

Pieces of meat, (often lamb or goat) and vegetables (such as carrots and potatoes) are cooked with hot stones. Water is added. The container, such as a pot, is covered to keep the heat in.

khorkhog

tsuivan

aarul

Aarul is a snack made of dried pieces of curds,

Usually made from the milk of nomadic cattle herds.

Borts is also dried, but this time it is meat,

Cut into strips or ground into powder, always ready to eat.

borts

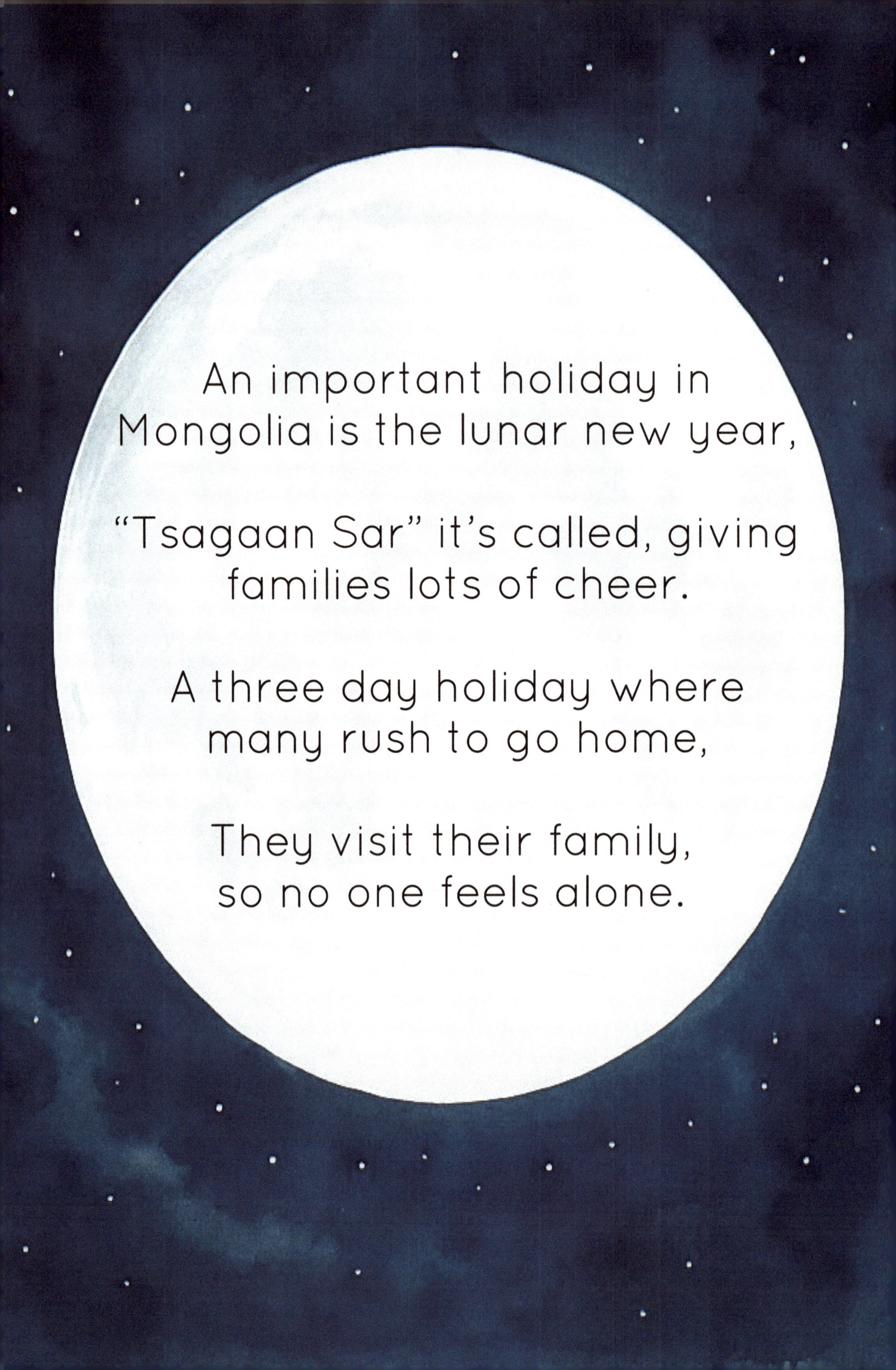

An important holiday in
Monopolia is the lunar new year,

"Tsagaan Sar" it's called, giving
families lots of cheer.

A three day holiday where
many rush to go home,

They visit their family,
so no one feels alone.

Blue scarves called "khadag" are given as a sign of respect, especially to older people. The blue represents the sky of Mongolia.

Naadam is a mid-summer festival of various fun and games,

Wrestling, horse racing and archery are the three main names.

A national holiday with contests all across the nation,

Watched throughout the centuries, a Mongol traditional celebration.

Money used in Mongolia is called the tugrik,

Long ago there was the dollar, but that changed pretty quick.

There were also coins and notes called the mongo,

But they too have gone, finished long ago.

The currency (money used) in Mongolia is called the tugrik. It is sometimes spelled togrog.

Long ago the mongo was used in Mongolia.

Mining in Mongolia earns the country lots of money,

As well as soft cashmere, those goats look pretty funny.

Adapted for their habitat, growing long hairs for winters of cold,

Shedding them when warmer spring comes, for cashmere they are sold.

Mining in Mongolia

Cashmere from goats

Throat singing began in the far and distant past,

Spreading across east Asia, it's something that has last.

In Mongolian throat singing is called "khoomei,"

Deep sounds that represent nature, it takes your breath away.

Khoomei (Mongolian throat singing) is used to sing urtiin duu (long songs).

Traditional music includes long
songs known as urtiin duu,

These tunes can last for minutes or
hours with words that are but few.

Morin khuur is a stringed instrument,
using horse hair or nylon instead,

A symbol of Mongolia,
known as the fiddle with a
horse's head.

Morin Khuur

Sukhbaatar Square in Ulaanbaatar is where the government does sit,

The parliament and president's offices are all able to fit.

Mongolia is not only about the capital of Ulaanbaatar,

There are more cities in this country, flung both near and far.

A statue of Ghengis Khan is in the centre.

Sukhbaatar Square, Ulaanbaatar

Erdenet and Darkhan are two places
in Mongolia's north,

The first of these has a huge mine,
copper it brings forth.

Darkhan in Darkhan-Uul Province
is a place of education,

A province is an aimag,
there are twenty-one in this nation.

A copper bowl

Map of Mongolia with Erdenet and Darkhan

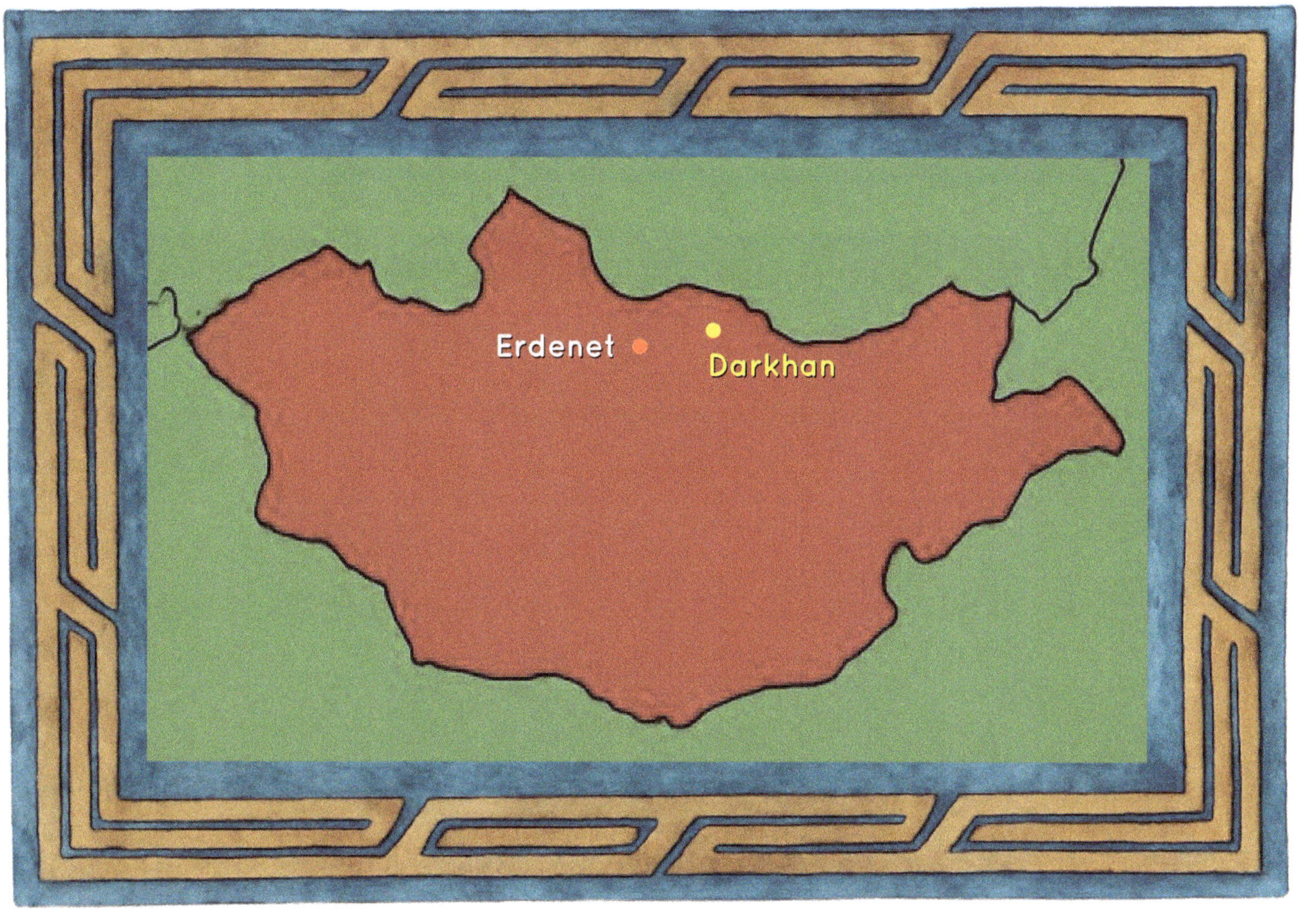

Map of Mongolia with its provinces - aimag

Buddhism in Mongolia,
there still is much to see,

In Kharkhorin, the medieval capital,
is the Erdene Zuu Monastery.

Or visit a temple destroyed and re-built, indeed a beautiful scene,

Erdene Khamba surrounded in summer,
by its magnificent colours of green.

The Buddhist symbol, ulzii, the never ending knot.

The Golden Stupa (a place where important items are kept and people meditate) at the monastery.

Erdene Khamba Temple

Монгол

Mongolian Cyrillic is how people do indeed write,

Borrowed from Russia, it's read from left to right.

Mongolian traditional script is read from the top to the bottom,

Taught again in the country, so the old ways aren't forgotten.

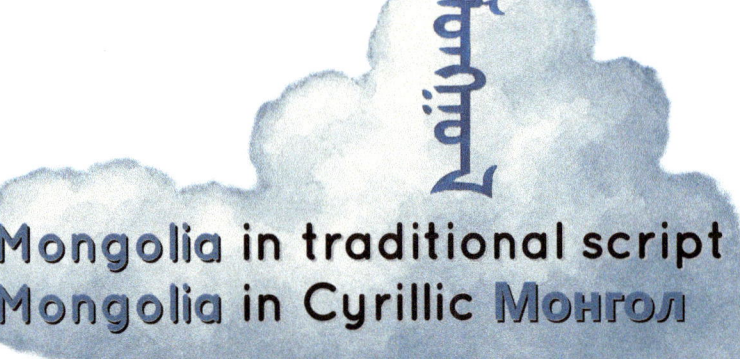

Mongolia in traditional script
Mongolia in Cyrillic Монгол

It's nearly the final chime of these
Mongolian facts of rhyme,

But one more piece of information,
It's not cold all the time!

Spring, summer, autumn and winter,
The colours are many, not few,

Adding to a land of eternal sky,
clear, deeply blue.

Spring and summer in Ulaanbaatar

The Tuul River in Ulaanbaatar in the autumn and winter.

Now really is the end,
it's been lots of fun,

Time to finish...
the rhyme is almost done.

"Sain baigaarai" (сайн байгаарай),
please stay well,

Time to leave, for now,
these fine things to tell.

Sain Baigaarai (сайн байгаарай) Stay Well

Bayartai (Баяртай) Bye

Acknowledgements

The title on the front cover uses Howdybun Regular font by Khurasan™
https://www.1001fonts.com/howdybun-font.html
Free for commercial use.
Howdybun is licensed under
https://creativecommons.org/licenses/by-nd/3.0/

The internal pages of the book uses Quicksand font by Andrew Paglinawan.
https://www.1001fonts.com/quicksand-font.html
Free for commercial use.
Quicksand is licensed under the SIL Open Font License (OFL)
https://openfontlicense.org/

The aimag (province) map on page 31 is based upon the map at -
https://commons.wikimedia.org/wiki/File:Mongolia_aimag_german.png
by Bogomolov PL who placed his own work in the public domain
Karte der Mongolischen Aimags, deutschsprachige Version
Mongolia aimag division map, German version

The illustrations in this book are based upon photographs taken in Mongolia and turned into watercolours.

www.ingramcontent.com/pod-product-compliance
Lightning Source LLC
Chambersburg PA
CBHW061403070526
44584CB00031B/4152